SEANNE N. MURRAY

The Art of Submission

The Woman's Guide to Fulfillment

SEANNE N. MURRAY

THE ART OF SUBMISSION

Copyright © 2019 Seanne N. Murray
All rights reserved.
**VIP INK Publishing Group, Incorporated
Atlanta, Georgia**

SEANNE N. MURRAY

And the day came when the risk to remain tight in a bud was more painful than the risk it took to blossom.

Anais Nin

PrintHouse Books, Atlanta, GA.

Published: 3-25-2019
ISBN: 978-1-7923-0535-1
LCCN: 2019936121

www.PrintHouseBooks.com

VIP INK Publishing Group; Incorporated

All rights reserved. No parts of this book may be reproduced in any way, shape, or form or by any means without permission in writing from the publisher, or the author, except by a reviewer.

SEANNE N. MURRAY

CONTENTS

		Page
	Acknowledgments	i
	Prologue	iii
	Introduction	v
1	Unlock the Cuffs: Free Yourself from Restraint	2
2	Remove the Mask: Let Go of Your False Self	10
3	Loosen the Corset: Accept All That You Are	19
4	Slip on the Stilettos: Walk with Confidence	29
5	Paint the Lips: Express Your Femininity	36
6	Pull the Chain: Take Control of and Share Your Life	43
7	Tickle Your Fancy: Live Your Best Life	47
8	A Final Note	52
	About the Author	54

SEANNE N. MURRAY

ACKNOWLEDGMENTS

When I started writing this book, I had a list of acknowledgements, people I wanted to confess my endless love and gratitude to. Of that list of 10 or so, only a few remain. Others did not exist in my world until now. Without diminishing the importance of the weighty impact that people have on our lives, I know, for sure, our lists will forever change. Change is the only constant there will ever be.

I wrote this book slowly, over several years, open to the gifts of allowing, knowing and transformation so that I could share through experience rather than conjecture.

The Art of Submission, The Woman's Guide to Fulfillment is my personal story of self-actualization and an illustration of self-reliance. It reminds us that, while we may love, love deeply, even obsessively, it is best to save that all-consuming love for ourselves. Always, is a word reserved for self. Without exception, life will show you repeatedly and consistently that you can always count on you.

THE ART OF SUBMISSION

PROLOGUE

Once I found myself at a meeting in a slinky bar (where most meetings are held in LA). I was navigating the delicate line of flirtation and business and allowing my peer to take an inappropriate liberty or two (like Bill Clinton testing the waters, a normal part of the game).

Another sip of my vodka on the rocks, a nod here, a head shake there, and then my adversary said, "You seem like a woman who needs a long leash." I gasped silently, and I wondered if he'd morphed into Pill Cosby or Harvey Weinstein.

I imagined an Amy Schumer/Joy Behar retort, my hand slapping his face, the remnants of my drink dripping down his cheeks in slow motion.

I'm no "50 Shades of Grey," virgin seeking sexual exploitation with a sociopathic narcissist, I thought.

"Okay, breathe. Remember the goal. Calm down," I said to myself.

Then, suddenly and shockingly, I slipped into the preverbal rabbit hole.

"A long leash, hmmm?" I considered it and pictured myself in a leather cat suit, my body the perfect replica of Halle Berry in Cat Woman.

"You know what? Yes, you are right! I do need a long leash," I responded.

After that meeting (and yes, I did close the business deal), his words continued to ring in my head.

You see, I've always been the good girl, the college virgin, the loyal date, the consummate professional, the non-complainer and here-to-please-but-not-on-my-knees negotiator.

Law school diploma in hand, I was once demur, slightly preppy and conservative, even with a strawberry tattoo etched onto my thigh by an ex-con in Philly.

Somehow, I was born knowing how to be good and how to follow direction. After, what felt like, a lifetime, good was no longer good enough for me or for those putting pressure on me to conform and subdue to their will. Good and all of the judgment that goes with it became boring, suffocating, demeaning. It was anesthetizing like Michael Jackson in Neverland or Prince dying in the "Let's Go Crazy" elevator. I thought I'd fall asleep and never wake up a la Lucy in the Sky With Diamonds.

THE ART OF SUBMISSION

No one forced me to endure the horror story I created, to accept a life of limitations, to marry someone who was no good for me, to take high-powered jobs that were exciting and simultaneously mind-numbing. I was the master of this distorted creation, the Stanley Kubrick of my time.

Knowing I could no longer live this way, that it was do or die, now or never, I locked a black leather collar securely around my neck, got the longest leash I could find and snapped myself into reality, into a life of my choosing. Nothing about my life was ever the same from that moment. I was reborn as if I'd baptized myself and my journey toward The Art of Submission began.

It is my deepest hope that you will join me, take hold of your own chain and enjoy life every single day.

INTRODUCTION

The Art of Submission began as a screenplay about an intelligent and attractive young woman named Sara, a born artist, who grows up suppressed by a domineering and demanding father dis-interested in her God-given talents and life purpose.

He allows her to "play" for a short period of time, until she's thirteen, and then all playthings are put aside. The tools of her art, she is a sketch artist and painter, are dismantled and violently destroyed by her father, it being time for stoic adulthood because, "get with the program", that's what life is.

Going forward, she's expected to please her father in ways appropriate (no flaws allowed) and sexually inappropriate, (he likes her to wear impeccably applied red lipstick to turn him on) no matter how you define it.

Her red painted lip mother (once the immaculate beauty) lives in denial, stuffing herself with brownies and daiquiris. She's way too convivial for her stodgy and anorexic, Opus One, drinking peers.

Sara follows the rules, her father's prescribed plan. She goes to law school, marries a doctor, albeit a dermatologist (not good enough as no one is ever good enough for Mom or Dad) and becomes a young law firm partner.

Her husband, much like her father, and to no surprise, comes from an abusive household, is narcissistic, insecure (my diploma is in a bigger frame than yours) sexually inept (his penis is smaller than most), awkward, and generally revolting. Through his insulting and offensive manner, he demands her subservience.

I won't ruin the story for you, but as with most creations, the screenplay is based loosely, and in part, on my perceived reality.

I call it an emotional autobiography, a story that highlights and is generated from the pain I felt, starting at seven years old, when I chose to shatter my own dreams, and leave my personal gifts behind to follow the accepted and predetermined path away from being my authentic self.

I was born an artist and believed I could change the world. I
wanted to be, and knew back then, that I was a writer, but writing was a hobby, not a skill, never a career, and not at all proper for a girl of my caliber.

I also wanted to be an archeologist.

One day I made the dreaded mistake of saying I wanted to be a pediatrician and from that point forward, all bets were off and medical school was the clear and precise goal.

I headed to college on a full academic scholarship with a fucking major in organic chemistry. I practically flunked the MCATs, which I refused to study for. Somehow, that morphed into law school (I did pretty well on the LSATs, but barely studied for those either), one acceptable profession taking the place of another, passed two state bars and all that (blah, blah, blah).

Next up was a career on Wall Street. I learned how to swear like a sailor, a skill I continue to enjoy today, fuck, and multi-task like a boss. That oddly culminated in the spiritless and prosaic world of medical education (the thought still makes me gag on a tongue depressor) and an equally vomit inducing marriage (more on that later).

I had a great resume and, at times, I felt good, but it was never enough, never satisfying or satiating.

It simply felt wrong.

I endured a sexless marriage lacking male essence. Changing light bulbs, car oil and water heaters became my second career. I chose a sociopathic, video game playing, ADHD stricken beast and ultimately a childless life.

My femininity was desecrated. How could I have children with a person I couldn't have an intimate conversation with?

To his utter surprise and dismay I refused to let him turn me into a sperm receiving, childbearing vessel.

Notably, initiating my divorce was the first real choice I'd made since I was seven, but it was a choice based on circumstance, consequence and need (a choice to make my body available to someone who might touch it, amongst other things), rather than a choice based on desire.

I felt a constant and unavoidable thirst for something more, a desire for the clarity, ease and sense of self I remembered so well from childhood.

That thirst built up over the years until the dehydration was mind numbing, blinding and heart breaking.

It took me another four years to reach the depths of the, oft noted, dark night of the soul.

I sank into the emptiness of my own guttural gasps. There wasn't enough wine in the world to quench or hide my longing for more.

It was time to jump into the ocean and either swim or drown, live or die.

Death would have been the easy choice, but who would take care of my dog, Harley? Regrettably, he's gone now, but I swear he saved my life. Living carried all the risk and all the glory. On one very specific day I chose life. I decided to embark on the journey back to my true self, toward my very real talents and potential. I decided to be the best seven-year old I could be and my entire world changed.

The purpose of this book is to reveal the steps necessary to become self-actualized, to tap into your divinity and be the extraordinary woman who was born into this world. The Art of Submission is all about being yourself all day every single day, submitting fully to who you really are and achieving your full potential.

I'll share the process I went through (without the wine), so that you can become the full expression of your authentic self, explore your deepest, often secret, desires and do what you were put on this earth to do (live and be happy).

I waited waaaaaaay too long and did it the hard way, (hard, not being a verb I'd ever use to describe my ex-husband) but you don't have to.

Get rid of the cuffs, the masks, the false restraints and perceptions, and anything else that may be holding you back from who you are.

I promise, you'll never think of "submission" the same way again.

THE ART OF SUBMISSION

THE ART OF SUBMISSION

Absolute liberty is absence of restraint; responsibility is restraint; therefore, the ideally free individual is responsible to him/herself.

Henry Adams

1 UNLOCK THE CUFFS

The first step in the Art of Submission is to Unlock the Cuffs or free yourself from restraint (handcuffs for fun will come later if you like).

It is the most difficult because it requires a conscious and definitive choice. It will not just happen.

Once you take this step, the path that follows will fall into place with surprisingly little effort because your desires will be clear and accessible and the Universe will conspire to help you.

Unlocking the cuffs requires deep, gut wrenching, investigation, evaluation, and evolution.

Change is often difficult and painful and this is no exception.

You have to find the key and unlock the cuffs on your own. No savior will help you. However, if you listen to yourself,

pay attention to the messages, primarily your own instinct and inner voice, you will find a way.

THE ART OF SUBMISSION

The cuffs are likely of your own making (not cute, pink and fuzzy), but defined by limitation, self-hatred or some other perceived and accepted self-lack.

They were likely latched onto your wrists by influencers like parents, teachers, or spouses. Perhaps they were bound to you by some group affiliation like race, sex or religion (the dominatrix of your choosing).

Regardless of the source, restraints, like most wounds, are self-inflicted (whether you buy them at the Pleasure Chest or the Dollar Store).

No one can force us to wear shackles without our consent.

Often, we choose to be bridled, controlled like animals (the cat woman costume was cute until it went too far) rather than opting to be the enlightened spirits that we are.

Don't be fooled, the life you are living is always, always,
always the life of your choosing.

As little girls, we're outspoken, demanding, unafraid, and without an ounce of self-consciousness (like the women on some raucous and raunchy comedy). Do you remember that and how much fun it was? I do and you can have that again.

You climbed, ran with abandon, fell off your bike, got dirty, got up, painted with mud and color, laughed and cried without covering your mouth, said what you meant, meant what you said and felt what you felt.

Then one day, someone, a parent, a teacher, an uncle said, "Always be a lady, sweetheart". Ladies don't scrape their knees or jump in the lake because it's hot af outside.

Ladies are pristine, well dressed (whatever the fuck that means) and speak when spoken to (Stepford Wives anyone?).

Boys have fun. Men run the world.

Ladies hold back. Ladies are reserved.

You've allowed yourself to be controlled by societal parameters, advisors and influencers.

Societal parameters appear in the form of definitions wrapped, like Saran wrap over our faces, in qualification, suppression and/or separation.

They are all methods of restraint orchestrated to keep us away from each other, ourselves and our feminine power.

We are conditioned based on the characterization and stereotypes we've been stamped with to arouse limitation and control.

Girls, in particular, are directed, at a young age, away from freedom and toward a form of servitude and subordination.

Women are told that if they act like a lady, receive proper training (like circus monkeys) and follow societal etiquette they can "think like a man" and achieve their dreams of being wifed up. On a side note, men advising women on how to behave? #no

Our advisors, parents, teachers and others, often, and with good intentions, guide us, influenced by their personal and painful experiences of rejection, depravation, and lack of self-worth.

Many adults are paralyzed by a veil of pain from their ancestors, tortured souls who survived slavery, the Holocaust, the Armenian genocide and any number of world atrocities, along with past and present-day racism, sexism and criminal and perverted behavior.

Flogger Alert: I'm not saying that history isn't important. I'm saying let history be history and stop using it as an excuse to be you! Let kids and/or adults, as the case may be, choose their future and create a new destiny, untethered.

Louis Vuitton trunk sized personal baggage is strapped and hanging on for dear life.

Let that shit go!

Our advisors taught us about every possible impediment, filling us in on the gory details, before we had a chance to experience them, in an effort to protect us.

Their desire to shield us was the genesis of the fear that's presenting itself now.

It's the dread (you don't want to get out of bed), the anger (you hate everyone and everything around us), the blame (none of it is your fault), the depression (you don't know if you want to live) and all of the other devastating thoughts and feelings that hold back the extraordinary woman within.

Media in the form of talk shows, magazines, news, rom com's, the learned ones on reality TV and social media pundits teach us how to be, how to catch a mate (bear trap assembly included), what to wear (on our not Kim K asses), what to say and how to say it so that we can complete ourselves with the ultimate match made in heaven.

For girls, the fairytale starts in the crib with Cinderella and Snow White, virginal women ripe for the peeling (green like Kiwi), born securely cuffed, ready to present their lock and key to the first rich, powerful man who looks their way (even if they beat them in an elevator a la your favorite NFL player or throw acid in their face, welcome to the Middle East).

These tawdry stories have evolved seamlessly into romance novels (the gentle maiden and the hunky long haired brute), feature films and Broadway plays (the prostitute shopping with her boyfriend's credit card on Rodeo Drive) and other irritating artistic expressions to reinforce unrealistic (read, fucking ridiculous and demeaning) stereotypes.

Fortunately for you, unlocking the cuffs begins the moment you drop the bullshit. They open (abra fucking cadabra) like magic.

Choosing to free yourself from the bogus imprisonment that confines you isn't easy, but it is critical. It's the first step against the false novelty of perfectionism and bondage, against what is socially accepted and expected.

It will be extremely painful (not like a beat down by a Housewife of choose your spot, probably NJ or Atlanta), but like shedding your own skin (a la Silence of the Lambs, sans Chianti), and it is utterly necessary for your survival.

HOW TO FREE YOUR SELF FROM RESTRAINT

The decision, in and of itself, to love and accept all that you are will begin the healing. The cuffs will fall away. The messages you receive by listening to your inner voice and paying attention to the world around you are the fuel you need to move forward.

1) Make the choice to love yourself above all else without compromise. Say "I am free" or simply "I am" out loud every morning and every evening and really let yourself feel it. Let the wisdom of who you are permeate your soul until it becomes irrefutable.

2) Accept that you are a limitless being, that there are no boundaries to who you are, that you are not your race, sex or any other classification. You are you. You are a powerful woman.

3) Pay attention. Listen and watch closely. Messages will be delivered in many forms. It may be in the hum of Bob Marley singing, "None but ourselves can free our minds" or a character in a Stanley Kubrick film saying, "The important thing is we are both awake now, and for a long time to come" or the voice of Lil Wayne saying "We're here to live. We're here to do, we're here to be" (yes, Lil Wayne has messages too).

SEANNE N. MURRAY

The most important kind of freedom is to be what you really are. You trade in your reality for a role. You give up your ability to feel, and in exchange, put on a mask.
Jim Morrison

2 REMOVE THE MASK

The second step in The Art of Submission is to remove the mask or let go of your false self, that persona you've invented to hide who you really are. Letting go of your false self requires that you recognize, accept and relish the real you, not who society obligates you to be or who your family or friends think you should be.

Part of letting go of your false self requires that you understand that you were born with the ability to nourish yourself and that you are self-sustaining.

You don't need or pay attention to encouragement or praise from others. Affirmation is a nice to have, not a need to have. Fulfilled women affirm themselves and their goals and their desires are clear.

They never settle for less than the highest expectation of
themselves.

We don't explain. We do.

We won't allow ourselves to be defined. We live fluidly, open to all possibility.

We do not seek to be desirable or coveted by others. We flourish on our own charms.

Flogger Alert: I'm not saying that human beings do not enjoy the affirmation, love and companionship of others. I'm saying you don't need it. It's not a necessity.

The love of another should never be greater than the love of self, and while it's wonderful to be understood, there's nothing more powerful than understanding and knowing ourselves.

As a lesson in what not to do, let's take a look at Snow White. I abhor fairytales in their current state and seek abolishment of the same (Let's start a change.org petition, shall we?).

Snow White's stepmother, the Queen, outrageously wicked and vain, is envious of Snow White's beauty and plots, multiple times, to kill her.

Snow White begs the huntsman for her life and breaks into a dwarf (is that even politically correct anymore?) dwelling for food. Not one, but seven dwarves welcome, rather than arrest her, and permit her to stay as long as she agrees to provide daily maid service (cause cleaning is what we do best).

Mind you, Snow White is aware that the Queen just tried to have her killed, but the Queen, disguised as a peddler selling lingerie (who made this up?) fools Snow White and tries to kill her again by corset asphyxiation (I swear, this is really how the story goes).

Low and behold, the seven dwarves come back in the nick of time, loosening the suffocating garment (probably a waist trainer), and saving her life.

Shortly thereafter, the Queen comes back again disguised as a farmer's wife, this time to serve up the poison apple. (Where does this chick get her amazing costumes and who's her makeup artist, the guy from Wakanda?)

Snow White eats the apple, seemingly dies, and is placed in a glass coffin.

The Prince sees her and wants her dead body delivered to his home (Necrophilia anyone?).

When the dwarves move the coffin, the apple is dislodged, (hallelujah!). Snow White awakens and she and the Prince live happily ever after, but not before brutally torturing the Queen to death. (Do we really wonder how little girls get messed up? Is this actually a bedtime story? Sweet dreams, bitches.)

Aside from the blatant stupidity and savagery of the Snow White story, the message that it delivers is that women need to be saved by men, by Princes, dwarves or even via accidents, but never, ever, ever (in my best Taylor Swift voice) deliberately, purposefully or intentionally through their own choice or will.

It's time to shake, shake the tree, get rid of all those apples and admit to yourself who you really are and then be that.

Are you funny, smart, joyful, relaxed, conservative, snarky (No one has ever called ME that.)? Be that!

Who's the person who lives in your thoughts? What are the conversations that play out in your mind that reveal what you really want to say, do and be?

Listen to the voice that speaks, but is rarely heard by others.

That's the real you, the fulfilled woman.

It's time to reveal the person you think no one will like because you're too something, too anything.

You will be brilliantly surprised by the reaction to that person you've been hiding.

People are drawn to honesty, openness, and fearlessness.

It's enough to live the non-fiction version of yourself.

It's time to kill the fantasy, become your own personal and personalized divine savior and fall deeply in love with who you are.

Once the mask is fully removed (if you have the Eyes Wide Shut Mask, save it for later) and you are revealed, the thought of covering or hiding yourselves in any way will seem repulsive and extreme.

Flogger Alert: The haters will show up for sure. They'll be everywhere, especially on social media if you choose to indulge. Take comfort in the fact that the 70-character bandits actually judge themselves most harshly of all.

Many will try to define or re-define you, try to put you back into the box you just barely crawled out of, the cage they still live in. It's cool to honor their place on the journey while staying true to yourself.

You will naturally begin to listen more than you speak, and hear with a resonance that did not previously exist.

It'll feel like a veil has lifted (like that time you married the wrong guy and thought what in the actual fuck) and you'll finally see the world with clear lenses.

The concept of us versus them will be gone.

The recognition of the amount of judgment there is in the world will be nauseating.

You'll lose your need to be understood.

Those who are willing and/or have the proclivity to listen, accept or help us will appear.

This step toward self-actualization is no joke and it will take time.

THE ART OF SUBMISSION

The mask you've been wearing was glued on. I'm not gonna lie, it will take effort to get rid of the imprint it leaves behind (It's way worse than going to bed with your makeup on, but easier than killing Jason in Friday the 13th), but it can be done. I promise.

Sometimes, you'll revert to old habits, but you'll recognize the old patterns more quickly over time. Eventually, that masked phantom will become a stranger to you.

You will know, definitively, what you like and don't like, what you want and don't want, what feels good to you and what
doesn't.

Your actions will move you toward well-being and pleasure. You will no longer be a self-imprisoned hostage.

You will not need to be saved by prince charming or open yourself to the destruction of an evil witch. You will sit calmly and decisively in the strength of your feminine power.

HOW TO LET GO OF YOUR FALSE SELF

The loss of the mask will be exciting and arousing as if seeing for the first time, unobstructed (like a virgin touched for the very first time. you're still hot, Madonna). You will see and be seen and live freely and unabashedly in your nakedness.

1) Audit your inner voice. Notice when thoughts or words make your body tighten or cause you to feel a sinking in your abdomen or pelvis. Those feelings of discomfort are your map, your path away from fraud, misrepresentation, deceit and disservice to yourself.

2) Let your concern about what others think of you fall away and revel in your own transparency (outside of a glass coffin).

3) As your views, opinions and vision for your life become clear, share them fearlessly without regard to the judgmental who will attack from a place of fear.

THE ART OF SUBMISSION

My happiness grows in direct proportion to my acceptance, and in inverse proportion to my expectations.

       Michael J. Fox

3 LOOSEN THE CORSET

The third step in The Art of Submission is to Loosen the Corset or accept all that you are.

This step in the process of submitting to your true self requires that you release self-judgment and the need to apologize for the masterpiece that you represent, the uniqueness you display, and the gifts you were born with and develop.

Fulfilled women don't apologize for who they are.

You already know what's hidden behind the closed door of your mind, heart and spirit.

You know what you were born with and why you are here.

You've been holding it in like some kind of Victorian debutante.

It's in that inner voice that speaks when you hear something that makes no sense, but don't say a word (shyly giggling and holding a tissue to your lips).

It's there when you're in a meeting listening to some nonsense and don't say a word in refute for fear of appearing aggressive (isn't that what they called Michelle Obama?).

It's clear when you think of an object that could be better (like sexier Spanxx), but do nothing about it.

It's evident when you dream about or envision something that's yet to be seen in this world (like clitoral training for men), but don't create it (I think someone tried that in San Francisco).

With every withholding, you are punishing yourself and the Universe. You are preventing the benefit of your exclusive, life changing, input, the very reason you were born.

As girls and women, we are constantly shushed, told to listen, not ask, to speak when spoken to. It's the epitome of ladylike behavior, appropriate like the muting of an R. Kelly song (#muteRKelly).

We are encouraged to mitigate our loquaciousness, gregariousness, and cleverness, often in an effort to make our male counterparts feel like comic book superheroes (extra points for ironing their capes).

THE ART OF SUBMISSION

Growing up, my father told me that "ladies always carry tissues in their pocket books" for themselves and others.

Even as a little girl, that suggestion zapped me like a dog breaking through an electronic fence! I wondered what fancy items men held in their pockets and which ones were there for my convenience.

The rebel in me has never carried a tissue in my bag (and I do not call my purse a pocket book, I mean, who says that?) since, though men have asked me for everything from Band Aids to nail clippers, but I digress.

The constant flow of messages you receive to inhibit yourself, to be the unbold, to be the supporters, rather than the originators and architects leads to a devastating result, the
murder (like an episode of How to Get Away with one) of our own fulfillment.

You are bursting (break into Katy Perry's Firework here) with insight, knowledge and innovation. When you suck all that in (like the latest faja or waist training devise), you live in constant and often excruciating pain.

If unattended, that sense of forced restraint results in depression, cutting, weight gain, hypertension, early signs of aging and so much more. I'm no doctor (to the great embarrassment of my family), but I know what I see, what I hear and what I've experienced.

Oprah (and now Dr. Phil) made a market out of interviewing women about the ruin and chaos of their lives, their cheating, sometimes gay, husbands, their disrespectful children, their loneliness, and their inability to forgive themselves based on their lack of self-worth.

Sucking it in or up (never mind the back fat rolling over the edges) is the worst you can do for yourself, your loved ones and society at large.

The introduction of new thoughts and ideas by us is crucial to our empowerment and growth, and to the expansion and improvement of the world.

By becoming a lover of exposure and change, you represent the full nature of womanhood and your ability to create and sustain life like no other.

Stop apologizing for who you are, what you've experienced or what you're capable of.

It is invigorating and expansive (ask Cardi B, shapely is in).

The more difficult it is, the more delicious (like taking off an underwire bra at the end of the day).

Initially, the exposure may feel uncomfortable, raw and even hurt (worse than a Brazilian wax).

Snakes don't die when they shed (assuming it's not for your new handbag). They are cleansed and rejuvenated.

THE ART OF SUBMISSION

Flogger Alert: Relax PETA! It's a joke.

Beware that self-approval tends to unclothe the bigoted, hateful and un-supporting around us (like the most unflattering image on a nude beach).

Not to be confused with narcissism, self-acceptance is the precursor to freedom. It rids us of un-useful debris and prevents stagnation.

Personal change is revolutionary, our way of evolving. The results are instantaneous and tangible.

The defects, hardships, and hindrances you're holding onto, like a Playboy Bunny wearing a lettuce wrap at a PETA convention (I swear, I love you PETA) are the keys to your brilliance.

Stop feeling sorry for yourself and embrace them!

They are the experiences needed to move forward and get on with the business of being you. They lead to and support your contribution and service to humanity.

Every open wound (like a bad waiter expecting a tip) is hoping to be adored, loved, exposed and healed.

Go ahead and rip off that Band-Aid (you already know I don't have one in my bag)!

The pain is temporary and there is nothing, I repeat, NOTHING, that you have endured, tolerated or withstood that hasn't already been experienced and overcome by someone else.

As you begin to share, you will let go of all embarrassment and self-consciousness.

Letting go will bring instant calm and comfort into your life. Share your story with others, those you trust and don't trust.

Share it with the biggest gossip you know (a la TMZ). Let your stories be carried like viral videos to friends, neighbors and unknowns. It doesn't matter because it doesn't matter what they think.

Whatever shame you were wearing like a life vest is gone now
and I promise you will not drown. To the contrary, you will thrive!

Whatever it was or they were, the rape, the abuse, the abortion, the bulimia, the binging, or the sexcapades, let them all sink like a fucking stone. It's time to say, fuck you to #metoo and hello to #iam.

Dare to risk full exposure for extraordinary rewards. Open your legs wide (like you're birthing a baby or having the best sex of your life, for those of us without children), and let the sun shine in.

Didn't that feel good? (if you didn't drip this time, maybe you will next time)

Notice how many others feel exactly the same way you do.

In disclosing and talking about your personal history, you'll begin to understand that pain and discomfort are the doors to opportunity, growth and enhancement.

They're gone now, those imaginary fears are no longer a
cloud above or inside you.

There's not a single secret left, nothing that anyone can ever hold against you (or bribe you for), nothing you can use as an excuse or reason to suppress or deny yourself.

Now you've advanced and are ready to stand, 4-inch heel, tall.

HOW TO ACCEPT ALL THAT YOU ARE

Strip yourself naked, completely bare, and dare to risk full exposure. The defects, hardships, and hindrances you're holding onto are the keys to your brilliance.

1) Assess, acknowledge and accept the experiences in your life, every sordid detail. Stop all waist training, sucking in or sucking up practices immediately.

2) Let go of embarrassment and self-consciousness, understanding that no experience is unique to you alone (everyone has back fat if the corset is too tight). Never apologize for who you are or what you've endured.

3) Share your story with others you trust and distrust, the bigger the gossip the better. Go viral with as many views as possible, Twitter, IG, FB if you're older, until there's not a single secret left, nothing that anyone can ever hold against you, nothing you can use as an excuse or reason to suppress or deny yourself. Enjoy that freedom, and then get on with the business of being yourself all day, every day.

SEANNE N. MURRAY

We gain strength, and courage, and confidence by each experience in which we really stop to look fear in the face... we must do that which we think we cannot.

Eleanor Roosevelt

4 SLIP ON THE STILLETOS

The fourth step in The Art of Submission is to slip on the stilettos, to walk with confidence.

Admittedly, high heels hurt, but they make us look good (says Christian Louboutin) and feel sexy, the feminine word for self-assured and courageous.

Though you're as provocative and fearless barefoot or in our Doc Martens, as you are in your red bottoms, I'm going to continue with the analogy.

This step in the process is not literally about walking in high heels, but about being self-possessed, resolute and determined.

Now that you're unrestrained, authentic and open, you can move forward being strong about who you are in all aspects of your life.

This is the time to make choices and take action.

Whether you're putting on work boots to start your own construction company, hitting the keyboard to be a writer, going back to school to become a physician, committing to the needs of children by creating or working for a foundation, the choice is yours and the world is truly your oyster (go for Venus on the Half Shell if you like), and has always been.

As I've alluded, you already know what it is that you want to do, that thing that's always been on your mind, but you were afraid to pursue.

Whatever it is, make yourself the full expression of it.

This is truly the road less traveled.

It may take Herculean (I'd love to use a Goddess name here, but to no surprise many were motivated by rage) strength.

It will be hard (remember those pinching shoes?) and it will be scary (it's easy to trip in 4-inch heels), but get up and keep going because there is nothing more important in your life
than this.

If that's not what you're feeling, then you're still in disguise, still hiding.

If that's the case, take a step back and stop reading.

You're not ready.

That's perfectly OK.

These things take time and everyone's journey is different.

If, on the other hand, this choice feels exciting, titillating, thrilling, and orgasmic (like that feeling between your legs on a first kiss), then you've found it!

It will make you lose sleep, distract you from other activities, fill your heart and possess your mind like a new lover.

Yes, it's that incredible. Even more wonderful than that is knowing that it's all yours, dependent on you and only you, meaning no one can take it away.

There'll be no unanswered texts, no Sex and the City style breakup on a post it note, no morning after pill. It's all on you, the good, the bad and the worst dressed at the Golden Globes.

In similar fashion to releasing your fears, start broadcasting what you really want. Speak it into existence with anyone who will listen.

I promise, the more you share it, the clearer it will become and the Universe will move with you to make it happen.

When you are alone, continue to speak, talk out loud about your mission and its conclusion.

What do you see? Describe it. How do you feel? What does it taste like, look like, smell like?

Do this every single day, at minimum in the morning and
evening.

The clearer you become, the more action you can take and the more the Universe will conspire with you to achieve your deepest desires.

So, move forward by any means necessary.

This is your life's mission, your destiny found, and the time to achieve the full manifestation of who you are and why you're here.

Work hard. Don't give up. Don't take no for an answer.

There will be many noes because when it's that important, the Universe wants to test you and people want to deny you.
You will even say no to yourself. Everything else will seem more important or appropriate. You'll categorize the thing you love, your destiny as a hobby, and all else as the real "work" you should be focused on.

It's a weird law, but it happens time and time again.

Greatness requires sacrifice, grit, guts and enormous courage.

Those heels may hurt like hell after hours of walking or standing, but there's no doubt they're the right size.

Read up on the law of attraction, stay positive and goal oriented and put in the work. Be a warrior (not reduced to a fucking "warrior princess"), a champion, a fighter, and a winner.

HOW TO WALK WITH CONFIDENCE

Now that you're unrestrained, authentic and open, you can move forward being strong about who you are in all aspects of your life. This is the time to make choices and take action.

1) If your choice feels exciting and you cannot, no matter what, no matter what is offered to you, put it aside, then you've found it! If not, take a step back and go back to Chapter 3. You're not ready.

2) In similar fashion to releasing your fears, start broadcasting what you want. Speak it into existence with anyone who will listen. When you are alone, continue to speak, talk out loud, about your mission and its conclusion. Become clear about what it looks, feels, tastes, sounds and smells like.

3) Ramp up your own courage in the face of societal or self-imposed norms. Be a warrior, not a princess!

THE ART OF SUBMISSION

SEANNE N. MURRAY

Beauty and femininity are ageless and can't be contrived, and glamour, although the manufacturers won't like this, cannot be manufactured. Not real glamour; it's based on femininity.

Marilyn Monroe

5 PAINT THE LIPS

The fifth step in The Art of Submission is to paint the lips or express your femininity, whatever that means for you.

You've accepted who you are and you're walking tall in the world of manifestation.

So, have a little fun, let your hair down, cut it off, or dye it purple. Painting the town red isn't just for Banksy anymore.

Allow that tingle to flow, the undeniable delicacy that is womanhood.

Contrary to popular belief, women are the most powerful beings on the planet. Betty White says, "Why do people say, "grow some balls"? Balls are weak and sensitive. If you wanna be tough, grow a vagina."

That's real strength!

Everything that's exciting about life, including life itself, comes through us.

THE ART OF SUBMISSION

We represent all creation. So, celebrate your power and your freedom.

There's nothing more exhilarating than self-appreciation, than walking through the world knowing that you are amazing and happy and strong and that the root of your joy, success and love comes from within.

Understanding that you are the orchestrator of your own life and feelings leaves others virtually powerless when it comes to controlling or altering your vision.

They will try (swinging in like Miley Cyrus on a wrecking ball) to take you down.

Often wearing a pin striped suit, or whatever the flavor of so-called boss wear happens to be at the time, they will seek to destroy your confidence.

Why? Because, either they have not submitted to themselves or they enjoy the game of subjugation.

They are holding onto dear life, male or female, by a thread, hoping they won't be found out, hoping you don't steal their thunder or expose their shame (like Jane swinging through the jungle after an escape from Tarzan).

They don't know that you don't even care, that you let go of judgment when you stopped judging yourself.

That's why you're glowing (eat your heart out Cover Girl)!

Basking in your own light, you feel better and look better in your bare skin.

You will be bold, pink and red, shining "bright like a Diamond" with Rihanna even as you "werk, werk, werk, werk, werk" your Fenty lipstick because now work is fun and fun is work.

You don't need boundaries or delineations. You're truly living now.

It's likely that, organically, you've started taking better care of yourself, eating right (try the sugar free life, I promise, you'll thank me), exercising, if only because damn, it feels good to be outside in that glorious sunshine.

Allow your inner voice to inform what's best for you, what foods are good for your health and well-being.

Enjoy the gifts of nature, the sun, the trees, and the ocean.

Let them soothe you like a universal meditation.

Painting your lips is the pièce de résistance, the cherry on top of that vegan, gluten free, sundae.

Hold onto that feeling on your own as long as you can.

Seduce and make love to yourself, figuratively and literally (yes, get that vibrator from Amazon).

Learn every succulent feature you have and enjoy the art of
exciting your mind, body and spirit all on your own.

Learn how to play by yourself, have personal parties, dance, drink wine, or tequila on the rocks (my drink of choice).

There's no such thing as celebrating too much when you're on your own. There's no one to be embarrassed around or hold back from. So, let it all out.

People will ask why you are so happy, what you're so positive about.

Tell them if you want, or not.

Remember, it's your playing field, your choice. You are no longer obligated to do, be or feel anything you do not desire.

It's likely that you'll want to shout from the rooftops when they ask and that's cool, but know that it will probably be a "parents just don't understand" scenario like Jada explaining to Will.

It seems so easy now, doesn't it?

You'll want everyone to make that decision and feel what you feel, but, as you know too well, it only happens when you're ready and thank all that is, you are ready.

HOW TO EXPRESS YOUR FEMININITY

Now that you're fully formed and living in the spirit of manifesting your true destiny, it's time to have some grown ass woman fun and experience the undeniable delicacy that is fulfillment.

1) Bask in the glow of your own light, even while being weary that others will try to pull you down into the doldrums you've left behind.

2) Take care of yourself. Feed your body what it needs, what your inner voice tells you is right for you and enjoy the spiritual and mental fruits of nature.

3) Discover and enjoy every part of your mind, body and spirit. Make love to yourself in every possible way, celebrate who you are on your own and do only what you desire.

SEANNE N. MURRAY

It is difficult to free fools from the chains they revere.
Voltaire

6 PULL THE CHAIN

The sixth step in The Art of Submission is to pull the chain or take control of and share your life. This step sounds exciting, but can be quite scary.

It's like leaving rehab for the first time, stepping out into the real world, a former addict, using your new skills to interact.

People will gravitate to the change, the natural glow, like honey, like giant wasps ready to sting, barnacles latching onto whales, or leeches wanting to suck the lifeblood out of us for their own use (Vampire Lestat, here they come).

When you walk into a room, people will see you, really see you because you exude transparency, exposure and fearlessness. You know exactly what you want and why you're here.

You'll become the drug, a psychedelic, no less, expanding the consciousness of all around you. It is essential not to allow anyone to take control of what you've worked so hard to free.

You'll be like a big, sleek, beautiful cat (pussy cat, if you will), ripe for the hunting, and you'll share yourself, but you must always hold your own chain, a chain without limits.

The Art of Submission, let's call it collaring just for fun, is a journey toward self-acceptance and you've achieved it.

The shift toward love and acceptance of yourself fully, completely and honestly has occurred.

When your leash is limitless, satisfaction comes from within.

When you acknowledge and then submit fully to who you truly are, you can fulfill your deepest desires and submission has begun.

So, tighten your collar, put on your extra-long leash, and run free! There are no more rules to follow.

SEANNE N. MURRAY

When we acknowledge and then submit fully to who we truly are, the powers of the Universe conspire to match our deepest desires.

        Seanne N. Murray

7 TICKLE YOUR FANCY

The seventh and last step in The Art of Submission is to tickle your fancy or enjoy your life without limitation or restriction.

This is gonna feel a little different, a little bit like the wind freeing your nipple in Central Park.

You know that favorite love song you swoon and groove to, when you get all up in your feelings with Drake, "Guess who's it is"? The answer is you, has always been you and will always be you.

You may not quite know how delicious this is, the experience of being completely and fully in love with yourself.

Women who love themselves don't wait.

There's nothing to wait for because you're already here.

Those unanswered texts, the calls that never were, the stalking his Facebook page, wondering what's up. Girl, I mean, woman, that is so far in your past you can't even taste it anymore.

The joy of being you, all of you, every day is everything.

You are independently fulfilled which means life moves in the flow, the self-created, unadulterated, they can't even begin to anticipate it flow.

You are the Oshun, the sun and your own moon.

Step into it with pink or black, the deal is, there is no lack, no hunger, no thirst. You, on you own, are a self-fulfilling prophecy.

Sometimes, you'll feel like you will burst.

Your body will be aligned with the spirit of all that is, and if someone comes along that interests you, who says he'll spin for you, humming T.I.'s "you can have whatever you like", let him in as long as he pleases you.

Love songs evolve from passion and heartbreak, from words that seam real, actions unfulfilled, but here's the real deal. Only you can dim your light, hollow out your heart, and take flight. When you fly, be a butterfly, jump out of that cocoon and throw it behind because you have arrived.

Appropriately, this chapter is last, because you have to be ready, learn the lessons of self-created heaven. No need for a man or anyone else to complete you, feed you (maybe tease you). Let go of the notion of what is right, don't get caught up, you are your own delight.

Forget men trying to schedule you in, making time for you or not, as if you are less than worthy. It'll make your heart and brain topsy turvy. I did that once upon a time in my own life, then realized the mistake was mine and like Maxine Waters, I started to reclaim my time.

Recognize this space as divine, never lose it and you'll be more than fine.

SEANNE N. MURRAY

THE ART OF SUBMISSION

I'm always making a comeback but nobody ever tells me where I've been.

Billie Holiday

8 A FINAL NOTE

As long as you shall live, this process will continue.

Just when you think you've hit the top of the mountain, from which there is no return, something will happen.

A trigger will be ignited.

A parent will die, a lover will break your heart, the economy will fail and you will fall into a sunken place deeper than Jordan Peele's Get Out. It'll probably feel worse than before now that you're aware of the full pleasure of fulfillment.

The good news is, you know the process. You've been there, done that, and like Cher, Madonna or Lady Gaga in their next iterations, you'll make a star is born comeback.

If you need to go all the way back, like Nike, just do it.

Like every billionaire who's gone bankrupt, and there are many, it'll be easier to recover.

You'll come out stronger, more dynamic and more vibrant than the first or last time.

Submitting to yourself is always the answer.

ABOUT THE AUTHOR

Seanne N. Murray, widely known as "SNM" and the architect of inspirational erotica, has been tantalizing and inspiring readers since 2014. Born in Detroit, raised in Westport, Connecticut and educated in Washington, D.C. and Philadelphia, SNM aspired to be a writer from the early age of seven. Distracted by her desire to please others and follow direction, she cultivated a successful business career which included becoming an esquire, not to be confused with escort, and enjoying the fruits of working on Wall Street. In 2001, following the terror she endured on 9/11, she experienced a profound inner transformation that triggered a radical change in the course of her life. Since then, she's been devoted to exploring and understanding the interconnectedness, or oneness, as she calls it, of humanity with a specific interest in women. The core of her expression is intense evaluation, self-acceptance and non-judgment, the prerequisites for intellectual, spiritual and sexual fulfillment. SNM is a nomad and claims no place of permanent domicile.

SEANNE N. MURRAY

SEANNE N. MURRAY

WWW.PRINTHOUSEBOOKS.COM

www.ingramcontent.com/pod-product-compliance
Lightning Source LLC
Chambersburg PA
CBHW032100150426
43194CB00006B/590

9781792305351